THE OFFICIAL
CRYSTAL PALACE
ANNUAL 2020

Written by Andrew McSteen
Designed by Matthew King Creative

A Grange Publication

© 2019. Published by Grange Communications Ltd., Edinburgh, under licence from Crystal Palace Football Club. Printed in the EU.

Photo Credits: PA Images (@paimages), Brickstand (@brickstand), Pinnacle Photo Agency Ltd (ppauk), Sebastian Frej, Neil Everitt (Crystal Palace FC), Tara Hook (Crystal Palace FC Women)

Thanks: Mike Pink, Terry Byfield, Harriet Edkins, Leanne Hides, Dan Blazer, James Woodroof, Matt Franks, Sharon Lacey (Crystal Palace FC), Grace Cullen, Robert Perrett (Palace for Life Foundation), Chris Smith (Brickstand), Tim Jotischky (PHA Group), Philip Mingo (Pinnacle Photo Agency Ltd)

ISBN 978-1-913034-17-7

CONTENTS

CLUB INFORMATION AND HONOURS

Full name: Crystal Palace Football Club
Founded: 1905
Nickname: The Eagles
Ground: Selhurst Park
Capacity: 25,486
Opened: August 1924
Address: Whitehorse Lane, London, England, SE25 6PU

ONLINE

Website: www.cpfc.co.uk
Palace TV: https://eagles.cpfc.co.uk
f www.facebook.com/officialcpfc
⊙ www.instagram.com/cpfc
🐦 www.twitter.com/CPFC
   www.dugout.com/CrystalPalace
▶ www.youtube.com/user/OfficialCPFC

HONOURS

› **Top-flight (currently Premier League)**
Best finish: Third - 1990/91
› **Second tier (currently Championship)**
Champions: 1978/79, 1993/94
Runners-up: 1968/69
› **Play-off winners:** 1988/89, 1996/97,
2003/04, 2012/13
› **FA Cup**
Runners-up: 1990, 2016
› **League Cup**
Semi-finalists: 1993, 1995, 2001, 2012
› **Zenith Data Systems Cup**
Winners: 1991
› **FA Youth Cup**
Winners: 1977, 1978
Runners-up: 1992, 1997

INDIVIDUAL RECORDS

APPEARANCES

› **Most senior appearances**
660 - Jim Cannon (1973-1988)
› **Most consecutive appearances**
254 - John Jackson

› **Youngest first-team player**
John Bostock - 15 years 287 days
(v Watford, 29th October 2007)
› **Oldest first-team player**
Jack Little - 41 years 68 days (v Gillingham, 3rd April 1926)
› **Longest serving manager**
Edmund Goodman - 18 years (1907-1925)

GOALS

› **Most goals scored (all competitions)**
165 - Peter Simpson (1929-35)
› **Most league goals in a top-flight season**
21 - Andrew Johnson (2004/05)
› **Most goals scored in a league game**
6 - Peter Simpson (v Exeter (H) 4th October 1930)
› **Fastest goal**
6 seconds - Keith Smith
(v Derby County (A) 12th December 1964)

INTERNATIONAL

› **Most capped international while at club**
Wayne Hennessey (Wales) - 39 caps (still at club)
› **Highest international goalscorer while at club**
Mile Jedinak (Australia) - 10 goals

CLUB RECORDS

› **Biggest home league win**
9-0 (v Barrow, 10th October 1959)
› **Biggest away league win**
6-0 (v Exeter, 26th January 1935; v Birmingham City, 5th
September 1987)
› **Heaviest home league defeat**
1-6 (v Millwall, 7th May 1927; v Nottingham Forest, 27th
January 1951; v Liverpool, 20th August 1994)
› **Heaviest away league defeat**
0-9 (v Liverpool, 11th September 1989)
› **Most consecutive victories**
17 (14th October 1905 – 7th April 1906)

RECORD ATTENDANCES AT SELHURST PARK

› **Top-flight:** 49,498 v Chelsea (27th December 1969)
› **Second tier:** 51,482 v Burnley (11th May 1979)

THE 2019-20 OFFICIAL CRYSTAL PALACE KIT

In the final match of last season against Bournemouth at Selhurst Park the new PUMA home kit for this season was revealed.

The home shirt includes the famous red and blue stripes of the Eagles, with a white collar, trim and faded pinstripe alongside the club's sponsor. The shorts are blue with a red trim and the socks are blue with a red band.

The Palace goalkeepers get to wear all-green, but don't lend your shirt to Vicente Guaita as he might just cut off the long sleeves!

The away shirt features a striking black design and the photos feature four of Palace's brightest talents: Luke Dreher, Nya Kirby, Sam Woods and Tyrick Mitchell, joined by Mamadou Sakho, Jeffrey Schlupp and Christian Benteke.

The 2013/14 and 2017/18 seasons also saw the Eagles wear a black away kit.

PALACE SQUAD 2019/20

GOALKEEPERS

13

WAYNE HENNESSEY

Country: Wales
Date of Birth: 24/01/1987
Signed: 31/01/2014 from
Wolverhampton Wanderers
Twitter: @WayneHennessey1
Instagram: @WayneHennessey
Did You Know?
Wayne has made the most international
appearances while a Palace player,
racking them up with Wales, including
making the semi-finals of UEFA Euro 2016.

31

VICENTE GUAITA

Country: Spain
Date of Birth: 10/01/1987
Signed: 01/07/2018 from Getafe
Twitter: @vguaita13
Instagram: @vguaita_13
Did You Know?
He likes to play in short sleeves and
always cuts his goalkeeper tops with
scissors.

19

STEPHEN HENDERSON

Country: Republic of Ireland
Date of Birth: 02/05/1988
Signed: 06/07/2019 free agent
(previously Nottingham Forest)
Did You Know?
His grandfather, father and two
uncles were all former professional
goalkeepers.

DEFENDERS

12

MAMADOU SAKHO

Country: France
Date of Birth: 13/02/1990
Signed: 31/08/2017 from Liverpool
Twitter: @MamadouSakho
Instagram: @MamadouSakho
Did You Know? Sakho originally joined
Palace on loan for the second half of the
2016/17 campaign under manager Sam
Allardyce to help the team avoid relegation.

3

PATRICK VAN AANHOLT

Country: Netherlands
Date of Birth: 29/08/1990
Signed: 30/01/2017 from Sunderland
Twitter: @PvanAanholt
Instagram: @PatrickvanAanholt
Did You Know?
He started his senior career at Chelsea
after playing for PSV Eindhoven's youth
side.

5

JAMES TOMKINS

Country: England
Date of Birth: 29/03/1989
Signed: 05/06/2016 from West Ham
United
Instagram: @TomkinsOfficial
Did You Know?
Tomkins played for Team GB's football
team at the London 2012 Olympic
Games.

THE GOALKEEPERS YOUNG GUNS:

> *Joe Tupper* > *Dion-Curtis Henry* > *Oliver Webber*

6

SCOTT DANN

Country: England
Date of Birth: 14/02/1987
Signed: 31/01/2014 from Blackburn Rovers
Twitter: @ScottDann6
Instagram: @ScottDann06
Did You Know?
Dann won the 2014/15 Player of the Year award and 2015/16 Players' Player of the Year award for Palace and has captained the team.

15

JEFFREY SCHLUPP

Country: Ghana
Date of Birth: 23/12/1992
Signed: 13/01/2017 from Leicester City
Twitter: @Jeffrey_Schlupp
Instagram: @JeffreySchlupp
Did You Know?
Schlupp won the Premier League title with Leicester City in the 2015/16 season, playing in 24 of their 38 league games.

34

MARTIN KELLY

Country: England
Date of Birth: 27/04/1990
Signed: 14/08/2014 from Liverpool
Twitter: @MartinKelly1990
Instagram: @MartinKelly_34
Did You Know?
Kelly joined home city club Liverpool at the age of seven and was called up by then England boss Roy Hodgson to his UEFA Euro 2012 squad.

24

GARY CAHILL

Country: England
Date of Birth: 19/12/1985
Signed: 05/08/2019 from Chelsea
Twitter: @GaryJCahill
Instagram: @GaryJCahill
Did You Know? Gary was a former England captain who received the armband for the first time for his country under future Palace boss Roy Hodgson. Cahill has won two Premier League titles, two FA Cups, one League Cup, one Champions League and two Europa League titles.

2

JOEL WARD

Country: England
Date of Birth: 29/10/1989
Signed: 29/05/2012 from Portsmouth
Twitter: @JoelWard2
Instagram: @JoelWard2
Did You Know?
Coming into the 2019/20 season, Ward is the longest-serving Crystal Palace player having been at the club since May 2012 and had the record number of Premier League appearances (167), four ahead of Wilfried Zaha (163).

THE DEFENDERS YOUNG GUNS:

> *Samuel Woods*
> *Ryan Inniss*
> *Nikola Tavares*
> *Tyrick Mitchell*
> *Jacob Mensah*
> *Lewis Byron*

MIDFIELDERS

4

LUKA MILIVOJEVIC

Country: Serbia
Date of Birth: 07/04/1991
Signed: 31/01/2017 from Olympiakos

Did You Know?
With 10 penalties scored last season, Palace captain Milivojevic became the second-ranked player in the all-time Premier League list for most in a season, equal with Steven Gerrard 2013/14, Frank Lampard 2009/10 and Alan Shearer in 1994/95. Top place is another Eagle – Andrew Johnson, with 11 in 2004/05. He signed a new contract at the beginning of this season, keeping him at the club until 2023.

7

MAX MEYER

Country: Germany
Date of Birth: 18/09/1995
Signed: 02/08/2018 free agent (previously Schalke 04)

Instagram: @MaxMeyer95

Did You Know?
Meyer part-owns a vegan food business back in his native Germany and won silver with his country at the Rio 2016 Olympic Games and gold at the 2017 UEFA European U21 Championship.

8

CHEIKHOU KOUYATE

Country: Senegal
Date of Birth: 21/12/1989
Signed: 01/08/2018 from West Ham United

Twitter: @PapiCheikhou
Instagram: @RoilionPapis8

Did You Know?
He played in the London 2012 Olympic Games for his country and claimed silver at the 2019 Africa Cup of Nations.

18

JAMES MCARTHUR

Country: Scotland
Date of Birth: 07/10/1987
Signed: 01/09/2014 from Wigan Athletic

Twitter: @JamesMcArthur16

Did You Know?
Former Scotland international McArthur won the FA Cup with Wigan in 2013, shocking Manchester City in the final.

44

JAIRO RIEDEWALD

Country: Netherlands
Date of Birth: 09/09/1996
Signed: 24/07/2017 from Ajax

Did You Know?
Riedewald was former manager Frank de Boer's first signing for Palace in a short spell which lasted just 77 days and five games – the shortest-ever managerial spell of games in the Premier League.

10

ANDROS TOWNSEND

Country: England
Date of Birth: 16/07/1991
Signed: 01/07/2016 from Newcastle United

Twitter: @Andros_Townsend

Did You Know?
He has won Crystal Palace's Goal of the Season Award twice – for 2016/17 with a strike against West Bromwich Albion and for 2018/19 with a wonder goal against Manchester City.

THE MIDFIELDERS YOUNG GUNS:

> *Luke Dreher* > *Giovanni McGregor* > *Nya Kirby* > *Jason Lokilo* > *Kian Flanagan*

VICTOR CAMARASA

23

Country: Spain
Date of Birth: 28/05/1994
Signed: 07/08/2019 from Real Betis (on season-long loan)
Twitter: @vicama8
Instagram: @vicama8
Did You Know?
He started his football career at the youth academy of hometown club Valencia CF in Spain – the same academy where Palace goalkeeper Vicente Guaita developed as a player.

JAMES MCCARTHY

22

Country: Republic of Ireland
Date of Birth: 12/11/1990
Signed: 07/08/2019 from Everton
Twitter: @JMcCarthy_16
Instagram: @jamesmccarthy90
Did You Know?
James McCarthy has a lot in common with Palace teammate James McArthur – they both played together at Scottish club Hamilton Academical and won the FA Cup with Wigan Athletic.

WILFRIED ZAHA

11

Country: Ivory Coast
Date of Birth: 10/11/1992
Signed: 02/02/2015 from Manchester United
Twitter: @WilfriedZaha
Instagram: @WilfriedZaha
Did You Know? Wilf originally joined Palace as a 12-year-old before making his debut five years later in March 2010. His form made him Sir Alex Ferguson's last-ever signing for Manchester United in January, but it was agreed to loan him back to the Eagles for the rest of the season to help the successful promotion push.

CHRISTIAN BENTEKE

17

Country: Belgium
Date of Birth: 03/12/1990
Signed: 20/08/2016 from Liverpool
Twitter: @ChrisBenteke
Instagram: @ChrisBenteke
Did You Know? Palace broke their club record transfer fee to sign the Belgium international in August 2016 when they paid Liverpool £27 million.

CONNOR WICKHAM

21

Country: England
Date of Birth: 31/03/1993
Signed: 03/08/2015 from Sunderland
Twitter: @ConnorWickham10
Instagram: @ConnorWickham21
Did You Know?
Wickham scored a header in the 2015/16 FA Cup semi-final to book the Eagles a final spot against Manchester United.

JORDAN AYEW

9

Country: Ghana
Date of Birth: 11/09/1991
Signed: 25/07/2019
Twitter: @Jordan_Ayew9
Instagram: @JordanAyew9
Did You Know?
Ayew originally moved to Selhurst Park on a season-long loan from Swansea City for the 2018/19 season before he was signed permanently last summer.

THE FORWARDS YOUNG GUNS:

> *James Daly* > *Brandon Aveiro*

Before this season the Eagles travelled to Switzerland for pre-season training and two friendly matches, against FC Luzern and BSC Young Boys. We take a look at the best shots from their trip.

ARSENAL
Nickname: The Gunners
Ground: Emirates Stadium
Capacity: 60,260
Built: 2006
Pitch size: 105m x 68m
Last Season: 5th in Premier League, 70 points
Premier League Head-to-Head: Played 20 Won 3 Drawn 4 Lost 13

ASTON VILLA
Nickname: The Villans
Ground: Villa Park
Capacity: 42,682
Opened: 1897
Pitch size: 105m x 68m
Last Season: Promoted as play-off winners of EFL Championship, 76 points
Premier League Head-to-Head: Played 14 Won 5 Drawn 5 Lost 4

AFC BOURNEMOUTH
Nickname: The Cherries
Ground: Vitality Stadium
Capacity: 11,329
Built: 1910
Pitch size: 105m x 68m
Last Season: 14th in Premier League, 45 points
Premier League Head-to-Head: Played 8 Won 2 Drawn 4 Lost 2

BRIGHTON AND HOVE ALBION
Nickname: The Seagulls
Ground: Amex Stadium
Capacity: 30,666
Built: 2011
Pitch size: 105m x 68m
Last Season: 17th in Premier League, 36 points
Premier League Head-to-Head: Played 4 Won 1 Drawn 1 Lost 2

Stats correct as of August 2019

BURNLEY

Nickname: The Clarets
Ground: Turf Moor
Capacity: 21,944
Built: 1883
Pitch size: 105m x 68m
Last Season: 15th in Premier League, 40 points
Premier League Head-to-Head: Played 8 Won 4 Drawn 1 Lost 3

CHELSEA

Nickname: The Blues
Ground: Stamford Bridge
Capacity: 40,853
Built: 1877
Pitch size: 103m x 67.5m
Last Season: 3rd in Premier League, 72 points
Premier League Head-to-Head: Played 20 Won 4 Drawn 2 Lost 14

EVERTON

Nickname: The Toffees
Ground: Goodison Park
Capacity: 39,221
Built: 1892
Pitch size: 100.48m x 68m
Last Season: 8th in Premier League, 54 points
Premier League Head-to-Head: Played 20 Won 5 Drawn 6 Lost 9

LEICESTER CITY

Nickname: The Foxes
Ground: King Power Stadium
Capacity: 32,273
Built: 2002
Pitch size: 105m x 68m
Last Season: 9th in Premier League, 52 points
Premier League Head-to-Head: Played 14 Won 8 Drawn 2 Lost 4

LIVERPOOL

Nickname: The Reds
Ground: Anfield
Capacity: 53,394
Built: 1884
Pitch size: 101m x 68m
Last Season: 2nd in Premier League, 97 points
Premier League Head-to-Head: Played 20 Won 5 Drawn 3 Lost 12

Stats correct as of August 2019

MANCHESTER CITY
Nickname: The Citizens
Ground: Etihad Stadium
Capacity: 55,017
Built: 2002
Pitch size: 105m x 68m
Last Season: Champions, 98 points
Premier League Head-to-Head: Played 18 Won 3 Drawn 4 Lost 11

MANCHESTER UNITED
Nickname: The Red Devils
Ground: Old Trafford
Capacity: 74,879
Built: 1909
Pitch size: 105m x 68m
Last Season: 6th in Premier League, 66 points
Premier League Head-to-Head: Played 20 Won 0 Drawn 4 Lost 16

NEWCASTLE UNITED
Nickname: The Magpies
Ground: St. James' Park
Capacity: 52,305
Built: 1892
Pitch size: 105m x 68m
Last Season: 13th in Premier League, 45 points
Premier League Head-to-Head: Played 16 Won 3 Drawn 5 Lost 8

NORWICH CITY
Nickname: The Canaries
Ground: Carrow Road
Capacity: 27,244
Opened: 1935
Pitch size: 104m x 68m
Last Season: Promoted as champions of EFL Championship, 94 points
Premier League Head-to-Head: Played 10 Won 2 Drawn 4 Lost 4

SHEFFIELD UNITED
Nickname: The Blades
Ground: Bramall Lane
Capacity: 32,702
Opened: 1855
Pitch size: 102m x 66m
Last Season: Promoted as runners-up of EFL Championship, 89 points
Premier League Head-to-Head: Played 2 Won 2 Drawn 0 Lost 0

Stats correct as of August 2019

SOUTHAMPTON

Nickname: The Saints
Ground: St. Mary's Stadium
Capacity: 32,384
Built: 2001
Pitch size: 105m x 68m
Last Season: 16th in Premier League, 39 points
Premier League Head-to-Head: Played 20 Won 3 Drawn 5 Lost 12

TOTTENHAM HOTSPUR

Nickname: Spurs
Ground: Tottenham Hotspur Stadium
Capacity: 62,062
Built: 2019
Pitch size: 100m x 67m
Last Season: 4th in Premier League, 71 points
Premier League Head-to-Head: Played 20 Won 3 Drawn 5 Lost 12

WATFORD

Nickname: The Hornets
Ground: Vicarage Road
Capacity: 21,000
Built: 1922
Pitch size: 105m x 68m
Last Season: 11th in Premier League, 50 points
Premier League Head-to-Head: Played 8 Won 3 Drawn 2 Lost 3

WEST HAM UNITED

Nickname: The Hammers
Ground: London Stadium
Capacity: 60,000
Built: 2011
Pitch size: 105m x 68m
Last Season: 10th in Premier League, 52 points
Premier League Head-to-Head: Played 16 Won 4 Drawn 5 Lost 7

WOLVERHAMPTON WANDERERS

Nickname: Wolves
Ground: Molineux Stadium
Capacity: 32,050
Built: 1889
Pitch size: 105m x 68m
Last Season: 7th in Premier League, 57 points
Premier League Head-to-Head: Played 2 Won 1 Drawn 0 Lost 1

Stats correct as of August 2019

WORDSEARCH

Can you find the names of all the Eagles' Premier League opponents? Find the words in the grid. Words can go horizontally, vertically and diagonally in all eight directions.

B	V	M	C	B	K	N	V	J	N	K	D	Q	X	T	H	J	K	Z	L	K
R	T	Y	P	G	W	E	S	T	H	A	M	U	N	I	T	E	D	F	R	D
I	N	L	T	Y	B	B	N	P	M	R	K	M	P	R	U	B	B	Z	R	T
G	Z	P	T	I	N	Y	U	T	G	N	Y	F	Q	D	O	G	S	M	U	Z
H	X	Z	M	Y	C	N	D	R	O	F	T	A	W	R	M	L	H	A	P	L
T	B	L	W	R	K	R	C	M	N	Y	T	N	M	V	E	V	E	N	S	R
O	L	N	L	N	S	H	E	K	R	L	L	G	R	K	N	R	F	C	T	B
N	P	Z	K	J	E	O	K	T	N	H	E	L	F	F	R	K	F	H	O	G
A	B	D	R	L	N	L	U	D	S	V	T	Y	R	Y	U	L	I	E	H	N
N	Z	R	S	F	Z	D	B	T	B	E	B	B	T	M	O	O	E	S	M	P
D	K	E	J	B	J	M	C	F	H	T	C	I	R	L	B	O	L	T	A	D
H	A	S	T	O	N	V	I	L	L	A	C	I	A	H	C	P	D	E	H	H
O	T	T	X	B	X	H	T	F	Q	H	M	N	E	L	F	R	U	R	N	T
V	Q	P	L	R	P	P	X	V	C	Y	E	P	L	L	A	E	N	C	E	H
E	L	V	L	J	R	X	W	I	D	S	M	W	T	P	C	V	I	I	T	C
A	T	T	L	T	B	O	W	X	R	N	G	C	T	O	K	I	T	T	T	T
L	P	T	M	Z	L	R	Y	A	T	Y	Q	N	F	H	N	L	E	Y	O	Z
B	G	Z	P	V	O	M	M	D	K	Y	M	L	Z	L	N	K	D	Q	T	D
I	P	V	E	N	Z	N	N	K	M	D	B	R	Y	N	O	T	R	E	V	E
O	H	S	X	B	L	N	E	W	C	A	S	T	L	E	U	N	I	T	E	D
N	N	R	M	A	N	C	H	E	S	T	E	R	U	N	I	T	E	D	N	C

AFC BOURNEMOUTH	LEICESTER CITY	SOUTHAMPTON
ARSENAL	LIVERPOOL	TOTTENHAM HOTSPUR
ASTON VILLA	MANCHESTER CITY	WATFORD
BRIGHTON AND HOVE ALBION	MANCHESTER UNITED	WEST HAM UNITED
BURNLEY	NEWCASTLE UNITED	WOLVES
CHELSEA	NORWICH CITY	
EVERTON	SHEFFIELD UNITED	

Answers on p61.

THE 2018/19 PREMIER LEAGUE SEASON IN NUMBERS...

MOST GOALS:
LUKA MILIVOJEVIC – 12

MOST CLEAN SHEETS:
VICENTE GUAITA – 7
[9TH OVERALL]

MOST ASSISTS:
JAMES MCARTHUR – 6

MOST SHOTS:
WILFRIED ZAHA – 73

AERIAL BATTLES WON:
JAMES TOMKINS – 91

TEAM TOTAL PASSES:
15,243

MORE 2018/19 STATS

Matches Played: 38
Wins: 14 (5 Home, 9 Away)
Draws: 7 (5 Home, 2 Away)
Losses: 17 (9 Home, 8 Away)
Points: 49
Position: 12th
Goals Scored: 51
Goals Conceded: 53
Goals Conceded per Match: 1.39
Hit Woodwork: 16 (4th Overall)
Team Clean Sheets: 12 (6th Overall)

Team Total Tackles:
730 (1st Overall)
Most Appearances:
James McArthur, Luka Milivojevic,
Andros Townsend – 38 (1st Overall)
Most Minutes Played:
Luka Milivojevic – 3,420 (1st Overall)
Most Passes:
Luka Milivojevic – 1,986
Most Touches:
Luka Milivojevic – 2,718

Most Tackles:
Aaron Wan-Bissaka – 129
(3rd Overall)
Clearances: James Tomkins – 182
Most Interceptions:
Aaron Wan-Bissaka – 84
Yellow Cards: 58
Red Cards: 2
Fouls: 224
Offsides: 78
Own Goals: 1

SEASON REVIEW 2018-19

AUGUST

SATURDAY 11 AUGUST 2018

FULHAM 0-2 CRYSTAL PALACE
Schlupp 41, Zaha 79

Jeffrey Schlupp and Wilfried Zaha scored to get the Eagles' Premier League campaign off to the perfect start with a 2-0 win over Fulham, who were returning to the Premier League after being promoted from the Championship.

MONDAY 20 AUGUST 2018

CRYSTAL PALACE 0-2 LIVERPOOL
Milner 45, Mane 90

The Eagles lost to Liverpool in their first home game of the season after a controversial penalty was converted by James Milner late in the first half. Aaron Wan-Bissaka was shown a red card in the 75th minute for bringing down Mohamed Salah before Sadio Mane sealed the win from a late counter-attack.

SUNDAY 26 AUGUST 2018

WATFORD 2-1 CRYSTAL PALACE
Pereyra 53,   Zaha 78
Holebas 71

Wilfried Zaha became Palace's all-time top Premier League scorer as his 24th top-flight goal passed Chris Armstrong's record, but it was not enough after Roberto Pereyra had curled a shot in before the break and Jose Holebas hit a cross-shot in after the break for Watford.

SATURDAY 1 SEPTEMBER 2018

CRYSTAL PALACE 0-2 SOUTHAMPTON

Ings 47, Hojbjerg 90

With a groin injury, Wilfried Zaha missed this match which saw new loan signing Jordan Ayew make his debut but ended with the Eagles' third Premier League loss in a row thanks to a Danny Ings strike just after half-time and an injury-time second from Pierre Hojbjerg, despite goalkeeper Wayne Hennessey making his first Palace penalty save, in the 63rd minute.

SATURDAY 15 SEPTEMBER 2018

HUDDERSFIELD TOWN 0-1 CRYSTAL PALACE

Zaha 38

Palace, wearing their yellow third kit for the first time, came away from home to win again thanks to a fantastic goal from Wilfried Zaha, who got the ball 40 yards from goal on the left wing and went past a number of Huddersfield players before whipping the ball in.

SATURDAY 22 SEPTEMBER 2018

CRYSTAL PALACE 0-0 NEWCASTLE UNITED

The first home win of last season nearly came in the rain at Selhurst Park as Mamadou Sakho missed a golden chance right at the end to grab three points with a header.

MONDAY 1 OCTOBER 2018

BOURNEMOUTH 2-1 CRYSTAL PALACE

Brooks 5,   *Van Aanholt 55*
Stanislas 87 (pen)

Another controversial penalty helped Bournemouth to victory over Palace despite left back Patrick van Aanholt equalising 10 minutes into the second half following an early goal from Bournemouth's David Brooks. The winner for the home side came from a late penalty after the referee ruled against Mamadou Sakho.

SATURDAY 6 OCTOBER 2018

CRYSTAL PALACE 0-1 WOLVERHAMPTON WANDERERS

Doherty 56

Selhurst Park had to wait yet another match to see the first home strike of the season as Premier League new boys Wolves scored early in the second half to grab all three points.

SUNDAY 21 OCTOBER 2018

EVERTON 2-0 CRYSTAL PALACE

Calvert-Lewin 87, Tosun 89

Roy Hodgson's side were undone by two very late goals from Everton substitutes Dominic Calvert-Lewin and Cenk Tosun, but it could have been so different had Cheikhou Kouyaté's header in the first half gone in, instead of hitting the crossbar and captain Luka Milivojevic's penalty had not been saved by England goalkeeper Jordan Pickford in the second half.

SUNDAY 28 OCTOBER 2018

CRYSTAL PALACE 2-2 ARSENAL

Milivojevic 45 (pen),   *Xhaka 51, Aubameyang 56*
83 (pen)

Luka led the way with two penalties to ensure his Eagles team grabbed a point against the North Londoners, but it could have been all three. After a first-half stoppage time penalty from Milivojevic, Arsenal went 2-1 ahead in the second half after a Xhaka free-kick and then the goalline technology telling referee Martin Atkinson that Aubameyang had squeezed the ball over the line. As Palace came back, Max Meyer hit the post but again Zaha won a penalty, fouled by Xhaka, and Captain Marvel slotted home for a point.

SATURDAY 1 DECEMBER 2018

CRYSTAL PALACE 2-0 BURNLEY

McArthur 16, Townsend 77

Palace got their first home league win of the season with goals from James McArthur and Andros Townsend. McArthur scored when his attempted cross went all the way into the goal while a sensational long-range strike from Townsend ensured the home fans left Selhurst Park happy. It was historic too as it was the Eagles' 100th win in the Premier League and 200th in the top-flight.

TUESDAY 4 DECEMBER 2018

BRIGHTON 3-1 CRYSTAL PALACE

Murray 24 (pen),   Milivojevic 81 (pen)
Balogun 31, Andone 45

Palace lost to 10-man Brighton at the Amex Stadium, who scored three times in the first half to stun Roy Hodgson's team. Former Eagle Glenn Murray scored a penalty but then Shane Duffy's red card appeared to put Palace in the driving seat, although it went the opposite way as shortly after Leon Balogun made it 2-0, and in first half stoppage-time, Florin Andone scored to put the game to bed despite a late Luka penalty.

SATURDAY 8 DECEMBER 2018

WEST HAM UNITED 3-2 CRYSTAL PALACE

Snodgrass 48,   McArthur 6, Schlupp 76
Hernandez 62, Anderson 65

Another three goals were conceded away from home as the Eagles lost to West Ham United at London Stadium even though Hodgson's men took an early lead through James McArthur. But an 18-minute spell in the second half saw West Ham take all the points with three goals.

SATURDAY 15 DECEMBER 2018

CRYSTAL PALACE 1-0 LEICESTER CITY

Milivojevic 39

Palace captain Milivojevic with time and space, decided to try his luck from 30 yards just before the break and produced a brilliant attempt that arced away from Kasper Schmeichel's dive and nestled inside the net in wet conditions.

NOVEMBER

SUNDAY 4 NOVEMBER 2018

CHELSEA 3-1 CRYSTAL PALACE

Morata 32, 65,   Townsend 53
Pedro 70

The Eagles came back from a first-half Alvaro Morata strike to equalise early in the second half through Andros Townsend after he was played in by James McArthur. But Morata struck again, on the end of an Eden Hazard free-kick and then five minutes later Pedro scored to make it 3-1.

SATURDAY 10 NOVEMBER 2018

CRYSTAL PALACE 0-1 TOTTENHAM HOTSPUR

Foyth 66

Another home game, another wait for a win as a Juan Foyth strike ensured Palace would leave the pitch disappointed as the Argentinian grabbed his first goal in English football in scrappy fashion after an Erik Lamela corner had seen a Harry Kane header blocked on the line.

SATURDAY 24 NOVEMBER 2018

MANCHESTER UNITED 0-0 CRYSTAL PALACE

Another scoreless game for the Eagles but it, and the point, was welcomed with open arms. Cheikhou Kouyaté had a goal ruled out for Palace minutes before the break, after he was given offside from a Milivojevic free kick, and at the end, Wayne Hennessey denied Romelu Lukaku with a save from his header.

SATURDAY 22 DECEMBER 2018

MANCHESTER CITY 2-3 CRYSTAL PALACE

Gundogan 27,   *Schlupp 33, Townsend 35,*
De Bruyne 85   *Milivojevic 51 (pen)*

It was the game which would prove to be unique – the Eagles became the only side all season to win at the Etihad Stadium in one of their best-ever Premier League performances, complete with an eventual Palace, and Premier League, goal of the season from Andros Townsend; a fizzing left-foot volley from 30 yards.

WEDNESDAY 26 DECEMBER 2018

CRYSTAL PALACE 0-0 CARDIFF CITY

The visiting side put in a heroic shift, repelling everything Palace could throw at them with former Eagles manager Neil Warnock taking a well-earned point back to Wales.

SUNDAY 30 DECEMBER 2018

CRYSTAL PALACE 0-1 CHELSEA

Kante 51

Palace ended 2018 with a defeat at the hands of Chelsea as N'Golo Kante's 51st-minute strike proved to be enough for the Blues to win in a match in which they enjoyed the better of the chances.

JANUARY

WEDNESDAY 2 JANUARY 2019

WOLVERHAMPTON WANDERERS 0-2 CRYSTAL PALACE

Ayew 83,
Milivojevic 90 (pen)

Palace loan striker Jordan Ayew scored his first goal for the Eagles as his strike in the 83rd minute was followed by a last-minute penalty from captain Luka Milivojevic in freezing temperatures.

SATURDAY 12 JANUARY 2019

CRYSTAL PALACE 1-2 WATFORD

Cathcart 38 (og)   *Cathcart 67, Cleverly 74*

A first-half Craig Cathcart Watford own goal could not be capitalised on by the Eagles as the Northern Irishman scored at the right end in the second half followed by a fine volley from Tom Cleverley.

SATURDAY 19 JANUARY 2019

LIVERPOOL 4-3 CRYSTAL PALACE

Salah 46, 75,   *Townsend 34, Tomkins 65, Meyer 90*
Firmino 53, Mane 90

The home side, going for the title, saw a narrow victory against the Eagles who had club legend Julian Speroni making his 404th start for the club in what would be his last-ever league game. Andros Townsend opened the scoring on 34 minutes in the first half before a lucky deflection landed in Mohamed Salah's path one minute into the second half. Firmino then put the home side 2-1 ahead with a deflected shot but James Tomkins headed in from Milivojevic's deeper corner, 2-2.

Unfortunately, a mistimed Speroni punch from a James Milner cross saw Salah poach to make it 3-2 and in a chaotic final few minutes, Milner saw red for a second yellow, Sadio Mane struck to make it 4-2 and then Max Meyer scored his first in a Palace shirt with 90+5 on the clock.

WEDNESDAY 30 JANUARY 2019

SOUTHAMPTON 1-1 CRYSTAL PALACE

Ward-Prowse 77   *Zaha 41*

An eventful evening for Wilfried Zaha saw the Palace man open the scoring but also sent off for two yellow cards as the Eagles drew 1-1 with Southampton at St Mary's with a second-half strike by James Ward-Prowse levelling things up.

FEBRUARY

SATURDAY 2 FEBRUARY 2019

CRYSTAL PALACE 2-0 FULHAM

Milivojevic 25 (pen), Schlupp 87

Palace completed the double over their west London rivals taking a big step to their Premier League security with goals from yet another Luka Milivojevic penalty, in the first half, and a tap-in from Jeffrey Schlupp at the end after good work from debutant, and Chelsea loanee, Michy Batshuayi.

SATURDAY 9 FEBRUARY 2019

CRYSTAL PALACE 1-1 WEST HAM UNITED

Zaha 76   *Noble 27 (pen)*

Wilfried Zaha returned from suspension to grab a deserved equaliser with a deflected shot in the 77th minute after a first-half Mark Noble penalty had put the visitors in front.

SATURDAY 23 FEBRUARY 2019

LEICESTER CITY 1-4 CRYSTAL PALACE

Evans 64   *Batshuayi 40,*
                    Zaha 70, 90,Milivojevic 81 (pen)

Palace took the lead against the run of play through Michy Batshuayi after James McArthur's shot had cannoned off the Belgian into the net, but Jonny Evans equalised shortly after the hour mark. However, Zaha, from a McArthur cross, put the visitors 2-1 up and then Luka Milivojevic made it 3-1 from the spot after Jeffrey Schlupp was fouled in the box. Zaha then made it 4-1 after being played through by Jordan Ayew.

WEDNESDAY 27 FEBRUARY 2019

CRYSTAL PALACE 1-3 MANCHESTER UNITED

Ward 66   *Lukaku 33, 52, Young 83*

Under the floodlights of Selhurst Park, Palace could not fight back after a Joel Ward header from a Jeffrey Schlupp cross had brought the Eagles within one of the Red Devils following two Romelu Lukaku strikes. But with the home side pressing for an equaliser late on, Ashley Young slotted home.

MARCH

SATURDAY 2 MARCH 2019

BURNLEY 1-3 CRYSTAL PALACE

Barnes 90   *Bardsley 15 (og), Batshuayi 48, Zaha 76*

Another impressive away performance saw the Eagles take another step towards safety with a 3-1 win in Lancashire that put them up to 13th in the Premier League table.

SATURDAY 9 MARCH 2019

CRYSTAL PALACE 1-2 BRIGHTON & HOVE ALBION

Milivojevic 50 (pen)   *Murray 19, Knockaert 74*

A frustrating clash played under the sun in SE25 saw rivals Brighton defeat the Eagles for the second time of the season with goals either side of a Luka Milivojevic penalty.

SATURDAY 30 MARCH 2019

CRYSTAL PALACE 2-0 HUDDERSFIELD TOWN

Milivojevic 76 (pen), Van Aanholt 88

Crystal Palace eventually secured all three points at a sunny Selhurst thanks to second-half goals from Luka Milivojevic and Patrick van Aanholt in a match which was part of the Premier League 'No Room For Racism' campaign and which, in the 13th minute, also saw a wonderful one-minute tribute in remembrance to former Palace Foundation player, Damary Dawkins, who sadly passed away at the age of 13 after a battle with Acute Lymphoblastic Leukaemia.

The breakthrough finally came in the 76th minute when Milivojevic again converted a penalty following a foul on Wilfried Zaha, his 10th league goal. Van Aanholt then scored late on after being teed up by Zaha.

APRIL

WEDNESDAY 3 APRIL 2019

TOTTENHAM HOTSPUR 2-0 CRYSTAL PALACE

Son 55, Eriksen 80

In this much-rearranged midweek fixture, Spurs finally played at their new stadium with an elaborate opening show and pre-match fireworks display followed by second-half strikes from a deflected Heung-Min Son shot and Christian Eriksen close-range effort.

SATURDAY 6 APRIL 2019

NEWCASTLE UNITED 0-1 CRYSTAL PALACE

Milivojevic 81 (pen)

This win ensured an 11-point difference between the Eagles and the foot of the table and it happened in what had become the 2018/19 season trademark, with the south Londoners, away from home, breaking against an offensive side to earn a penalty through Wilfried Zaha, converted by captain Luka Milivojevic. This came with 10 minutes remaining and followed first-half 'goals' ruled out for both sides, and despite seven minutes of additional time, the Eagles were not to be denied.

SUNDAY 14 APRIL 2019

CRYSTAL PALACE 1-3 MANCHESTER CITY

Milivojevic 81   *Sterling 15, 63, Jesus 90*

Eventual champions Manchester City impressed in a 3-1 win thanks to two from Raheem Sterling and a late finish from Jesus as they felt the pressure from Liverpool going into the final stretch. A Luka Milivojevic free kick had brought the home side within one but despite a late surge Kevin De Bruyne set up Gabriel Jesus to slot home from close range in the 90th minute to end any chance of the Eagles earning a point.

SUNDAY 21 APRIL 2019

ARSENAL 2-3 CRYSTAL PALACE

Ozil 47,   *Benteke 17, Zaha 61, McArthur 69*
Aubameyang 77

Another memorable 3-2 away victory last season came at the Emirates Stadium, the first win at the stadium for an away side in the league since August 2018. On his 200th Premier League appearance, Christian Benteke scored after heading in from a Milivojevic cross and was later denied a second in the first half with an offside call. The second half saw Arsenal come back through Mezut Ozil but Wilfried Zaha beat his man to shoot home and make it 2-1, running off into celebration with the Eagles' fans caught in the blazing sun nearby and they had more to celebrate moments later when James McArthur headed home following a Scott Dann header.

SATURDAY 27 APRIL 2019

CRYSTAL PALACE 0-0 EVERTON

A quiet game saw Palace and Everton cancel one another out to finish the match with a point each – another one on the way to an Eagles' club-record points total in the 20-team Premier League era.

MAY

SATURDAY 4 MAY 2019

CARDIFF CITY 2-3 CRYSTAL PALACE

Kelly 31 (og), Reid 90   Zaha 28, Batshuayi 39, Townsend 70

Palace faced the Welsh side fighting for their Premier League survival, but goals from Wilfried Zaha, Michy Batshuayi and Andros Townsend ensured the Eagles were the ones who could breathe easy at the end, with their win confirming Cardiff's relegation to the Championship.

Zaha's strike was his 10th goal of the Premier League season and marked his best-ever season in front of goal for Palace.

SUNDAY 12 MAY 2019

CRYSTAL PALACE 5-3 BOURNEMOUTH

Batshuayi 24, 32,   *Lerma 45, Ibe 56, King 73*
Simpson 37 (og),
Van Aanholt 65, Townsend 80

Selhurst Park said goodbye to Julian Speroni and Jason Puncheon on the pitch after this season finale which had eight goals in an unexpected blockbuster of a match. Palace, playing in their newly-unveiled 2019/20 home shirt scored first, through Michy Batshuayi who then doubled the home side lead with Bournemouth making it three thanks to an own goal.

The second half saw the visitors pull back two before Patrick Van Aanholt settled Selhurst nerves (4-2). Joshua King then scored to make the difference one, but Andros Townsend ensured the win with 10 minutes remaining.

Palace history was made as VAR was used for the first time at Selhurst Park with referee Martin Atkinson showing Grimsby defender Andrew Fox a red card after just two minutes for a foul on Andros Townsend. The game was one to forget though until Jordan Ayew scored late on with his header home in front of the near 20,000-strong crowd.

LEAGUE CUP

TUESDAY 28 AUGUST 2018 (CARABAO CUP, SECOND ROUND)

SWANSEA CITY 0-1 CRYSTAL PALACE
Sørloth 70

The Eagles went through to the third round of the league cup after Alexander Sørloth struck home in the 70th minute in south Wales.

TUESDAY 25 SEPTEMBER 2018 (CARABAO CUP, THIRD ROUND)

WEST BROMWICH ALBION 0-3 CRYSTAL PALACE
Townsend 6, 81, Van Aanholt 76

Andros Townsend scored twice to help put Palace into the fourth round of the league cup either side of a Patrick van Aanholt goal.

WEDNESDAY 31 OCTOBER 2018 (CARABAO CUP, FOURTH ROUND)

MIDDLESBROUGH 1-0 CRYSTAL PALACE
Wing 45

The Eagles made the long trip up to the north-east only to lose against former manager Tony Pulis and his Middlesbrough side in the last 16 thanks to a strike from Lewis Wing.

FA CUP

SATURDAY 5 JANUARY 2019 (FA CUP THIRD ROUND)

CRYSTAL PALACE 1-0 GRIMSBY TOWN
Ayew 86

SUNDAY 27 JANUARY 2019 (FA CUP FOURTH ROUND)

CRYSTAL PALACE 2-0 TOTTENHAM HOTSPUR
Wickham 9, Townsend 34 (pen)

Former Spurs academy player Andros Townsend sealed a win for Palace with a penalty to move into the fifth round with his strike making it 2-0 following an early goal from Connor Wickham – his first in over two years after starting for the first time in 26 months.

And, in what would be his final game for the Eagles, goalkeeper Julian Speroni was impressive, making an amazing double-save at the end of the first half and ending perfectly as he broke the club's all-time clean sheet record with his 112th shutout, overtaking Nigel Martyn.

SUNDAY 17 FEBRUARY 2019 (FA CUP FIFTH ROUND)

DONCASTER ROVERS 0-2 CRYSTAL PALACE
Schlupp 8, Meyer 45

Palace moved into the FA Cup quarter-finals after a Sunday win over the League One side thanks to two goals at either end of the first half with Jeffrey Schlupp firing in from across the box inside the first 10 minutes and then Max Meyer's additional time header from an Andros Townsend cross sealing the victory.

SATURDAY 16 MARCH 2019 (FA CUP QUARTER-FINAL)

WATFORD 2-1 CRYSTAL PALACE
*Capoue 27, Batshuayi 62
Gray 79*

Despite early attacking efforts, the Eagles crashed out of the FA Cup one game from a Wembley semi-final. Vicente Guaita was caught out by a Watford cross which fell at the feet of Etienne Capoue who finished into an empty net to make it 1-0 but the second half saw Michy Batshuayi bring the scores level to launch Vicarage Road into life with the game immediately injected with the passion and energy of 3,000 vociferous south Londoners.

But it was not to last as Watford, who would go on to lose 6-0 to Manchester City in the FA Cup Final, regrouped and struck again through substitute Andre Gray to confirm their passage.

PALACE HEROES: JULIAN SPERONI

Record-breaking goalkeeper Julian Speroni left the Eagles at the end of last season after nearly 15 years of service.

From 2004-2019 the Argentinian won the Player of the Season Award four times and was part of a number of momentous events in the history of the club, seeing it progress from relegation in his first season to securing a seventh consecutive year of Premier League football in his 15th.

Speroni played 405 times for the Eagles, the fourth-highest in Palace history and the most of any goalkeeper. His final match saw him keep a clean sheet – one of 112 in his Palace career – against Spurs in the FA Cup Fourth Round in January 2019.

Thanks for the memories Manos de Dios (Hands of God).

THE BEST

The 2018/19 season Crystal Palace FC Awards were held in front of a packed-out Boxpark in Croydon with the entire men's and women's first team squads in attendance, signing autographs and celebrating successful seasons.

Crystal Palace Player of the Season:

AARON WAN-BISSAKA

Crystal Palace Players' Player of the Season:

AARON WAN-BISSAKA

Crystal Palace Goal of the Season:

ANDROS TOWNSEND

Crystal Palace Under-18 Player of the Season:

MALACHI BOATENG

Crystal Palace Women's Player of the Season:

ASHLEE HINCKS

Crystal Palace Under-23 Player of the Season:

KIAN FLANAGAN

Chairman's Award for Outstanding Contribution:

JULIAN SPERONI

PFA Community Champion Award:

AARON WAN-BISSAKA AND CIARA WATLING

PREMIER LEAGUE GOAL OF THE SEASON:
ANDROS TOWNSEND

For Palace fans, Christmas came early last year on 22 December as not only did the Eagles beat champions Manchester City away, they witnessed the official Premier League goal of the season when Andros Townsend hit a 30-yard volley into the net to make it 2-1 to the Eagles in the 35th minute in a game they would go on to win 3-2.

The goal also won the Goal of the Season award at the Crystal Palace FC End of Season Awards, with 91% of the total vote, in addition to the 2018 Goal of the Year award at the London Football Awards and the Premier League's Goal of the Month award for December.

"It was the sweetest strike of my career."

"It was the sweetest strike of my career," said the forward. "I don't think I will ever hit a ball as sweet as that again. It was a special, special day for everyone connected with Crystal Palace to go to Manchester City and get three points against the champions.

"Everything about the game, the opponent, the strike it was perfection, I think a strike like that was needed to beat the champions away from home. I'm thankful it dropped nicely for my left foot, I struck it clean and the rest is history.

"I don't know how I managed to hit it that perfectly from that far out, but I get such a sense of pride every time I watch it and it seems to get better and better."

DESIGN YOUR OWN PALACE MATCHDAY PROGRAMME

Crystal Palace FC's Content and Production department produces an official matchday programme for every first team home match at Selhurst Park every season. It comes as a printed version and a digital version.

The programme includes all the latest information about the whole club along with interviews, pictures, statistics and lots more.

Last season there were 22 home games so 22 editions were produced and here they all are…which one is your favourite?

EAGLE EYE

Photographer Dan Weir covers everything from first-team to Academy matches for Palace and is a passionate, lifelong Eagles fan. He picks out his top seven photos from last season and explains what is happening and why they are important to him.

CREDIT: @PPAUK

1 ROCKETMAN DELIVERS

My favourite shot from last season is the Premier League Goal of the Season from Andros Townsend at Manchester City to put Palace 2-1 ahead. What an unbelievable moment to capture and I don't believe many other cameramen managed to grab the shot, which made it all the better.

3 WICKHAM BAGS UNDER SELHURST LIGHTS

Managing to score against Tottenham Hotspur in the FA Cup, Connor Wickham's goal celebration is one of pure relief after his comeback from injury.

2 JOY AT THE EMIRATES

Palace's team goal celebration from Arsenal away as the players all jumped on James McArthur after his goal put us 3-1 up.

Michy Batshuayi celebrates against Leicester City away with a nice knee slide straight down the lens.

4 SCHLUPP TAKES FLIGHT

Jeffrey Schlupp's goal celebration away against Manchester City after scoring to pull Palace to 1-1, starting the road to victory in the 3-2 win at the Etihad Stadium.

Wilfried Zaha's goal celebration after scoring to put Palace 3-0 ahead.

ZAHA'S LEAP OF JOY

Wilf's goal celebration on his own: jumping in the air after scoring to put Palace 2-1 ahead away at Arsenal.

Premier League U15 Super Floodlit Cup

THE CRYSTAL PALACE FC ACADEMY TEAMS

The Crystal Palace FC Academy continues to produce superstar players with Wilfried Zaha and Aaron Wan-Bissaka the latest two to play for the first team.

In total, the club has 10 academy teams with some managed by former Palace players like Richard Shaw, Paddy McCarthy and Darren Powell. They are the U9s, U10s, U11s, U12s, U13s, U14s, U15s, U16s, U18s and U23s.

The academy is based opposite the first team training ground in Beckenham, and the U23s sometimes play at Selhurst Park and are allowed to feature up to three over-age players which means players from the first team who are new or returning from injury can play!

Last season Darren Powell's U15 team won the Premier League U15 Super Floodlit Cup.

HOW TO...
DRIBBLE WITH WILFRIED ZAHA

Last season, Wilfried Zaha had the most attempted dribbles in the Premier League with 249 attempts – only Chelsea's Eden Hazard (now at Real Madrid) completed more dribbles (138) than Zaha (113).

Zaha also won the most penalties with six, meaning a total of 15 won since the 2013/14 season, equal with Leicester City's Jamie Vardy and one behind Manchester City's Raheem Sterling, on 16. Since that season he has also attempted the most dribbles by any player – 1,331.

SO WHAT IS HIS SECRET?

"I used to play in South Norwood on a little five-a-side concrete pitch and when you're playing in smaller, tight areas, you need to think quickly what you're going to do, what skill you're going to use to get past the person. I am a skilful player and that is what my whole game is based on. I live off nutmegs. So when you bring those skills on to a pitch, it's a lot easier because you've got a lot of space.

"Also, I used to practice ball control all the time at home with a tennis ball and played a game against my little sister where I tried to dribble around her, and she tried to get the ball with her hands. It's much harder when someone is trying to get the ball from you with their hands.

"For me, it was all about building up technical skills and expressing yourself – it was tunnel vision, determination and sacrifice with what I wanted to do, and nothing could distract me. I was doing what I loved and too tired when I got home to do anything else."

KAYLA THE EAGLE

If you have ever visited Selhurst Park you may have seen a spectacular Bald Eagle flying around – but do not worry, it's only Kayla!

Kayla has been the 'Official Live Mascot' of the Eagles since 2010 and when she is in attendance at home games she spends time meeting fans outside before going inside to fly from one end of Selhurst Park to the other just before kick-off and again at half-time.

Originally from Canada, Kayla resides at the Eagle Heights Wildlife Foundation charity based in Eynsford, Kent and which is open to the public.

CRYSTAL PALACE FC
WOMEN

Crystal Palace FC (Women) was founded in 1992 and the team is a large part of the Crystal Palace FC family.

They have three senior squads: First Team, First Team Reserves, Development Team, eight junior teams (U16 Academy, U16 Reds, U15s, U14 Academy, U14s, U13s, U12 Academy and U12s) and four mini teams (U11s, U10 Academy, U10s and U9s).

Players from both the men's and women's teams attend community events together with Crystal Palace FC providing financial, marketing and other support.

The senior team plays in the FA Women's Championship as Crystal Palace FC, and with women's football in England continuing to grow attendances increased by around 50% last season at their home ground Bromley FC. They also played at the famous Selhurst Park!

First team players from the men's side have also been very supportive with Bakary Sako, Mamadou Sakho and Wilfried Zaha all watching games – Wilf even made a financial contribution to support the development of the women's first team which is semi-professional with the players all having other day jobs.

THE PALACE MASCOTS

PETE AND ALICE THE EAGLE

Pete and Alice the Eagle are the Official Crystal Palace FC Mascots who have been keeping fans of all ages entertained at Selhurst Park for many years.

Pete wears Number 19 on his back and Alice Number 05. Together they are '1905' – the year the club was founded.

Can you think of any other birds which can be found at Premier League clubs?

SPOT THE BALL

There are too many balls in play! Can you work out which is the real one?

A ☐   B ☑   C ☒

D ☒   E ☐

Answer on p 61

CLUB AND

MANY OF THE PALACE SQUAD HAVE
REPRESENTED NATIONAL TEAMS
AT VARIOUS LEVELS. THE EAGLES
CAN EVEN BOAST THEIR OWN FIFA
WORLD CUP WINNER – ENGLAND'S
NYA KIRBY, WHO WON THE U17
COMPETITION IN 2017.

Nya Kirby - England

Wayne Hennessey - Wales

Mamadou Sakho - France

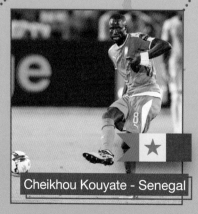

Cheikhou Kouyate - Senegal

Christian Benteke - Belgium

COUNTRY

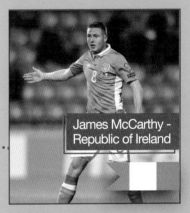

James McCarthy - Republic of Ireland

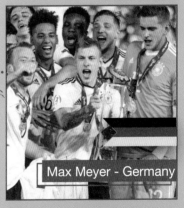

Max Meyer - Germany

Wilfried Zaha - Cote d'Ivoire

Luka Milivojevic - Serbia

Patrick van Aanholt - Netherlands

DEVELOPING THE FUTURE

Looking to the future, Palace manager Roy Hodgson named seven young Development players in his squad for the pre-season Uhrencup tournament in Switzerland where they played games against BSC Young Boys and FC Luzern. The youngsters went on to play in other pre-season matches against Nottingham Forest, Bristol City, Bromley, Dulwich Hamlet and AFC Wimbledon.

LUKE DREHER

Central midfielder Dreher made his full professional debut against Bournemouth on the final day of last season after being named in the first team squad for the Manchester United Premier League game and Middlesbrough League Cup match. In 2015/16 he was named the U18 Player of the Season and also featured in the first team pre-season ahead of the 2017/18 season.

This pre-season Dreher played the first 45 minutes against Luzern before coming on for James McArthur in the last five minutes against Young Boys. He played 84 minutes against Barnet, came on as an 81st-minute sub in the 5-0 win away at Bristol City and played all 90 minutes against AFC Wimbledon.

SAM WOODS

Central defender Woods, who started off as a right back, made his professional debut in that Middlesbrough League Cup game last season and regularly travels with the senior squad. He is a lifelong Palace fan and played all 90 minutes against Luzern and Barnet. He came on as a sub for Scott Dann against Young Boys and was an unused sub against Nottingham Forest before playing the full 90 minutes against AFC Wimbledon.

NYA KIRBY

Kirby, who won the U17 World Cup with England in 2017, struck home the eventual winner for Palace in the penalty shoot-out win against Luzern after coming on as a 65th-minute sub. The confident penalty was not surprising, seeing as he scored the winner in England's last 16 match against Japan on the way to the title back in 2017. He was the youngest squad member in Switzerland.

JAMES DALY

A talented, traditional left-footed centre forward, Daly spent much of last season on loan to Isthmian League Premier Division club Kingstonian before playing for the Palace U23 side and earning a contract extension in SE25. Daly came on as a 65th-minute substitute against Luzern and then played all 90 minutes against Barnet. He was on the bench for the first team friendly against Nottingham Forest ahead of playing the first 45 minutes against Bromley and all 90 against AFC Wimbledon.

TYRICK MITCHELL

Left back Mitchell signed for Palace from Brentford at the end of the 2015/16 season and regularly trains with the first team, awaiting his first call-up to the squad. He signed a new deal in January 2019 and played 35 minutes against Luzern.

NIKOLA TAVARES

Another player who joined the Eagles from Brentford, left-footed centre back Tavares has made an impression already in SE25, sitting on the bench for the final game of last season against Bournemouth. Born in South Africa to a Portuguese father and Croatian mother, Tavares has represented Croatia at U18, U19 and U20 level and signed a new deal last July. He appeared for the first half in the draw against AFC Wimbledon.

KIAN FLANAGAN

Winner of the U23 Player of the Season award last season thanks to his 10 goals from midfield, Flanagan made his U23 debut at just 15 years old and also represented the Republic of Ireland at U19 level. He played 18 minutes against Luzern, and 79 minutes against Barnet with his corner kick setting up Connor Wickham for Palace's second goal. He also featured for the whole second half against Bromley and final 11 minutes against AFC Wimbledon.

ORIGINS

THE CRYSTAL PALACE FOOTBALL TEAM

RUSSELL

In 1851 the 'Great Exhibition' took place in London and an enormous glass structure was built in Hyde Park to accommodate all the exhibitors from around the world.

After it had finished the structure was moved to Sydenham Hill to continue to be used, hosting the FA Cup Final between 1895-1914.

In 1905 Crystal Palace Football Club was formed at the venue which was locally referred to as 'The Crystal Palace' and the club was given 'The Glaziers' as a nickname. A glazier is someone very skilled with working with glass.

The new club Crystal Palace FC played their first-ever match against Southampton Reserves at the Crystal Palace on 2nd September 1905 after entering Southern League Division Two.

Despite losing 4-3 in that game, 'The Glaziers' did not lose another game in the 1905/1906 season and finished as champions.

If you look very carefully at the Palace badge, you can see an outline of the old 'Crystal Palace' building, which burnt down in a fire in 1936.

CLUB CREST

1940s – 1955, 1955 – 1972

We have had a club logo, or crest ever since the late 1940s which featured an image of the Crystal Palace building with a claret and blue shield on the front – the same colours as our kit then. In 1955, a new badge came in with a white and black image of the large glass building and the words 'Crystal Palace F.C.' underneath.

1972 – 1980s

In 1972, the club held a competition among fans, allowing them to decide how the club's badge would look. The winning design saw a large red ring carrying the letters 'CP' in the centre. The words 'Crystal Palace F.C.' also featured, as did the club's nickname at the time, 'The Glaziers'.

1980s

Soon after, another new badge was designed with a large eagle perched on a football, with the name of the club and image of the Crystal Palace featuring.

1980s – 2013

In the 1980s another redesign happened which lasted until 2013, although the Eagle was changed in 1994.

2013 – PRESENT

The current badge was designed with the 1973 crest in mind with the towers, glass building and eagle all featured.

Even though badges were not used on kits until the 1940s, nowadays they are used on merchandise, matchday programmes, signage around the stadium and much more.

SINCE BEING FORMED IN 1905 MANY PLAYERS AND MANAGERS HAVE CALLED CRYSTAL PALACE FC HOME.

HERE ARE...
THE RECORD BREAKERS!

MOST SENIOR APPEARANCES

JIM CANNON
660 • (1973-1988)

MOST CONSECUTIVE APPEARANCES

JOHN JACKSON
254

YOUNGEST FIRST-TEAM PLAYER

JOHN BOSTOCK
15 YEARS 287 DAYS
(v Watford, 29th October 2007)

LONGEST SERVING MANAGER

EDMUND GOODMAN
18 YEARS • (1907-1925)

MOST GOALS SCORED
(all competitions)

PETER SIMPSON
165 • (1929-35)

MOST LEAGUE GOALS

PETER SIMPSON
153 • (1929-35)

MOST GOALS IN A SEASON
(all competitions)

PETER SIMPSON
54 • (1930/31)

RECORD HOLDERS

MOST LEAGUE GOALS IN A SEASON

PETER SIMPSON
46 • (1930/31)

MOST LEAGUE GOALS IN A TOP-FLIGHT SEASON

ANDREW JOHNSON
21 • (2004/05)

MOST GOALS SCORED IN A LEAGUE GAME

PETER SIMPSON
6 • (v Exeter (H) 4th October 1930)

MOST GOALS SCORED IN THE FA CUP

PETER SIMPSON
12

MOST GOALS SCORED IN THE LEAGUE CUP

MARK BRIGHT
11

MOST HAT-TRICKS SCORED
(all competitions)

PETER SIMPSON
20

FASTEST GOAL

KEITH SMITH
6 SECONDS
(v Derby County (A) 12th December 1964)

MOST CAPPED INTERNATIONAL WHILE AT CLUB

WAYNE HENNESSEY
39 CAPS • (Wales)

HIGHEST INTERNATIONAL GOALSCORER WHILE AT CLUB

MILE JEDINAK
10 GOALS • (Australia)

PALACE HEROES:

GARETH SOUTHGATE

GARETH SOUTHGATE

OBE

Midfielder/defender Gareth Southgate came through the Palace academy, youth and reserve teams to become a first team regular, eventually making 191 appearances in total for the Eagles between 1990-1995, scoring 22 times. In his career with Palace, Southgate played full-back, centre-back, sweeper and in the middle or right side of midfield.

At 22 years old and just after he had passed 100 appearances for the club, Southgate was made captain when he took the armband for the Division One away victory at Barnsley in November 1993. That 1993/94 season saw one of his proudest footballing moments when he lifted the Division One Championship Trophy at Selhurst Park at the end of the season, celebrating a return to the Premier League as the youngest Palace captain to win promotion or championship title.

Southgate left Palace at the end of the 1994/95 season and moved on to have a successful playing career with Aston Villa, Middlesbrough and England, before retiring and then managing Middlesbrough, England U21s and the England senior squad where he excited a country, guiding the Three Lions to the semi-finals of the 2018 FIFA World Cup for the first time since 1990 and having Southgate London Underground tube station temporarily renamed 'Gareth Southgate' in his honour.

Gareth regularly returns to Selhurst Park to watch the next crop of England players.

THE CRYSTALS – OFFICIAL CHEERLEADERS FOR CRYSTAL PALACE FC

Since 2010, 'The Crystals' have been performing at Selhurst Park, contributing towards creating the unique atmosphere inside the stadium, which is widely recognised as one of the best in the Premier League.

Before the match and during half-time at home games the semi-professional dance group perform specially-choreographed routines as well as meeting and greeting fans outside and inside Selhurst Park.

In addition to their matchday work, The Crystals are ambassadors for the club and the local community, raising substantial amounts of money for good causes throughout the year.

The Crystals were the first 'NFL-style' cheerleaders in sport in the UK and come from a mixture of backgrounds including nurses, entertainment managers, teachers, florists, law students, full-time mums, city workers, admin staff, retail and full-time professional dancers.

You can follow them on their social media channels…

 CrystalsCPFC   **@Crystals_CPFC**   **@TheCrystalsCPFC**

Local lad and Palace legend Wilfried Zaha went back to his old school last season as part of the work the Palace for Life Foundation does in the local community.

The Foundation is the official charity of Crystal Palace FC which has been working with the south London community for over 25 years and uses the power of football and Palace to change the lives of people across south London, particularly the most hard-to-reach and hard-to-help.

Wing-wizard Wilf went back to Whitehorse Manor in Thornton Heath where he also did a quiz with the pupils and was shown a poem he had written at the school which is just a short walk away from Selhurst Park!

WILFRIED ZAHA: "WHAT A DAY! THANKS TO EVERYONE AT WHITEHORSE MANOR FOR WELCOMING ME BACK. LOTS OF HAPPY MEMORIES AND A WONDERFUL EXPERIENCE SEEING THE KIDS AND MY OLD TEACHERS."

YEAR 4 PUPIL ABOUT WILF: "IT WAS REALLY INSPIRATIONAL! IT SHOWED ME THAT EVEN THOUGH YOU COME FROM A SMALL PLACE, YOU CAN STILL ACHIEVE BIG THINGS!"

WHITEHORSE MANOR HEAD TEACHER NINA ACHENBACH: "IT'S BEEN REALLY WONDERFUL HAVING WILF BACK AT THE SCHOOL AND IT'S BEEN TRULY INSPIRATIONAL FOR EVERYONE."

ALL THE MOVES

Palace for Life Foundation, the Premier League and the BBC joined up for 'Super Movers', which brings stars from the worlds of football, music and television together in fun, free and easy-to-follow videos to help everyone get active.

Palace players Christian Benteke, Patrick van Aanholt, Ciara Watling and Jordan Butler appeared with pupils from Oasis Academy Ryelands to star in a video for the 'Eagle Swoop', an easy-to-copy dance invented by pupils from the school, which is close to Selhurst Park.

The pupils also performed the dance in the Fanzone at Selhurst Park on a matchday with the video now forming a big part of Palace for Life's Healthy Eagles campaign, shown at primary schools across south London, encouraging everyone to join in and be active.

Find out more information about the Palace For Life Foundation through their social media channels...

@PalaceForLife

PALACE AROUND

Even though we are SOUTH LONDON and PROUD! Crystal Palace FC has fans all across the world – some have even set up their own football clubs called Crystal Palace!

Let's have a look at where the global Eagles are!

• • • • • • • • • • • • • • • • • • •

NORTH AMERICA

Fans in North America also had an opportunity to watch Palace live in person when the squad toured in the USA and Canada in July 2016. The Eagles played Philadelphia Union, FC Cincinnati and Vancouver Whitecaps in three games under then manager Alan Pardew. The squad even trained at the home of American Football team, the Cincinnati Bengals from the NFL!

Crystal Palace even had a club in the USA. From 2006-2010 Crystal Palace Baltimore played in the USL and USSF leagues.

Canada: CPFC Canada, Golder Horseshoe Glaziers (Ontario)

USA: Austin Eagles
Boston Eagles
Chicago Palace
Colorado Palace
CPFC Buffalo
CPFC Cincinnati
CPFC Fresno
CPFC Houston
CPFC Madison
CPFC Minnesota
CPFC New Jersey
CPFC San Diego
CPFC San Francisco
CPFC Syracuse
Crystal Palace Atlanta
Crystal Palace Washington DC
Dallas/Fort Worth Palace
Detroit Eagles
Maine Eagles
Milwaukee: CPFCMKE
NY Eagles
Philadelphia Palace
Pittsburgh Palace
Richmond Eagles
South Florida Palace
USA: CPFC in the USA

THE WORLD

EUROPE

Faroe Islands: CPFC Faroe Islands
Germany: German Eagles
Ireland: Irish CPFC
Italy: Crystal Palace Italia
Norway: CPFC Norway
Poland: CPFC Polska
Spain: Iznajar Eagles
Sweden: Crystal Palace FC Sweden
Switzerland: CPFC Switzerland
Turkey: Istanbul: CPFC Turkey
Scotland: Crystal Haggis SC

OCEANIA

Countrywide: CPFC Australia Network
Adelaide: CPFC Adelaide
Melbourne: CPFC Melbourne Supporters Club
Sydney: Crystal Palace Sydney Supporters

ASIA

One Sri Lankan fan who used to live near Selhurst Park returned home to live and loved the club so much he set up Crystal Palace FC Gampola in 2007, and they are now one of the top clubs in the Sri Lankan top division with some of their players even making the national team!

Hong Kong: CPFC Hong Kong
These supporters actually got to see the Eagles in Hong Kong at the 2017 Premier League Asia Trophy where they met the players and even had a selfie with Chairman Steve Parish!

Japan: CPFC Japan | **UAE:** Dubai Eagles

Photos from supporters' club social media

LEGO PALACE

Chris Smith is a big Lego fan and a big Crystal Palace fan – so what better to do than combine the two?

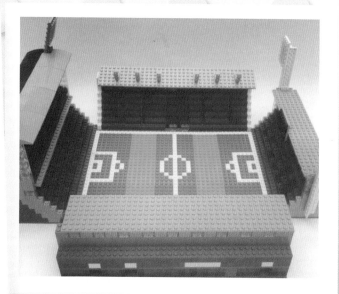

His love of the Eagles, and of the building blocks, led him to want to recreate all 92 English football league grounds – starting with Selhurst Park as part of his 'Brickstand' project.

He starts with getting lots of pictures of the grounds from the internet then using Google Maps to see all the different angles. Then, like all of us, he uses trial and error to build the stadiums.
Chris has also recreated some famous Crystal Palace moments using minifigures too...

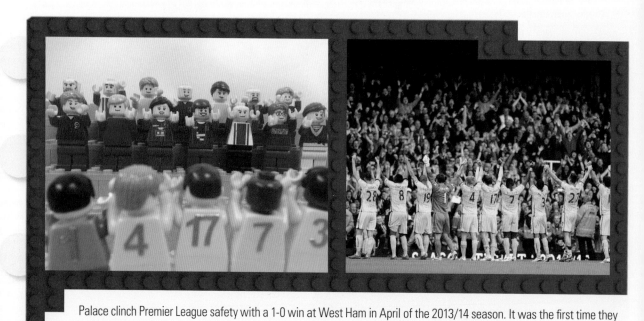

Palace clinch Premier League safety with a 1-0 win at West Ham in April of the 2013/14 season. It was the first time they had avoided relegation in any of their four previous Premier League seasons, sparking these celebrations between players and fans.

Striker Kevin Phillips scores the winning penalty in extra-time of the 2013/14 Championship Play-Off Final against Watford at Wembley to send the Eagles up to the Premier League.

Palace captain Geoff Thomas raises the Zenith Data Systems Cup at Wembley Stadium in April 1991 after the Eagles beat Everton 4-1 after extra time.

After coming on as a substitute in the 64th minute following an amazing recovery from injury, Ian Wright put Palace 2-1 up in the 1990 FA Cup Final against Manchester United. Here, he slots in his second goal in extra time to make it 3-2, but Mark Hughes would equalise late on as United salvaged a 3-3 draw.

Chris uses 1,500-2,000 pieces for each stadium

› **After four years, Chris is halfway through the 92 grounds**
› **He created 'Brickstand FC' nicknamed 'The Builders' who play at Brick Lane**
› **Brickstand FC 'play' matches on Twitter against teams like 'Blockport County' and 'Atletico Buildbao'**
› **Follow Brickstand on Twitter: @brickstand**

HOW TO...TAKE PENALTIES WITH
LUKA MILIVOJEVIC

Palace captain Luka Milivojevic was the only Premier League player to reach double figures in penalties scored last season when he scored 10 times.

Those 10 strikes from 12 yards out put him equal with Premier League legends Steven Gerrard, Frank Lampard and Alan Shearer in reaching double figures for penalty goals, but one short of the record in a single season – held by Eagles legend Andy Johnson in the 2004/05 season, with 11. The Serbian international talks through the perfect penalty…

"WHEN WE GET A PENALTY, IT'S MY JOB TO SCORE."

"PENALTIES ARE NOT A LOTTERY, THEY ARE A LOT OF FOCUS, CONCENTRATION, QUALITY AND TECHNIQUE."

"YOU NEED TO CARE ABOUT EVERYTHING THAT IS IMPORTANT FOR A PROFESSIONAL FOOTBALL PLAYER; FOOD, RECOVERY, HOW YOU LIVE AND HOW MUCH YOU REST."

"I WATCH VIDEOS OF GOALKEEPERS AND TRY TO SCOUT THEM."

"I PRACTICE, NOT FOR A LONG TIME, BUT REGULARLY. NORMALLY THE DAY BEFORE A GAME AND I DECIDE THEN WHICH WAY I WILL SHOOT. I MAKE MY MIND UP DURING THE WEEK AND 99% OF THE TIME I NEVER CHANGE."

"IN THE END IT ALL DEPENDS ON ME: HOW I SHOOT – THE GOALKEEPER HAS NO CHANCE IF I SHOOT HOW I WANT AND WHERE I WANT."

"IT IS NOT ALWAYS EASY, ESPECIALLY IN THE LAST 10-15 MINUTES OF A GAME WHEN YOU'RE GETTING TIRED AND YOU WANT TO KEEP FOCUSED."

"EVERYONE LIKES TO TRY AND SHOOT IN SOME UNIQUE WAY, TO HAVE THEIR OWN STYLE, BUT WHEN YOU'RE OLDER AND YOU'RE EXPERIENCED, YOU KNOW WHAT WORKS."

"WHEN YOU'RE OLDER, YOU SEE WHAT IS MORE IMPORTANT, YOU HAVE MORE EXPERIENCE AND YOU ARE CALMER."

"TODAY, PENALTIES HAVE BECOME LIKE MIND GAMES."

WORDFIT

CAN YOU FIT THESE PAST PALACE MEN'S AND WOMEN'S PLAYER OF THE YEAR AWARD WINNERS INTO THE GRID?

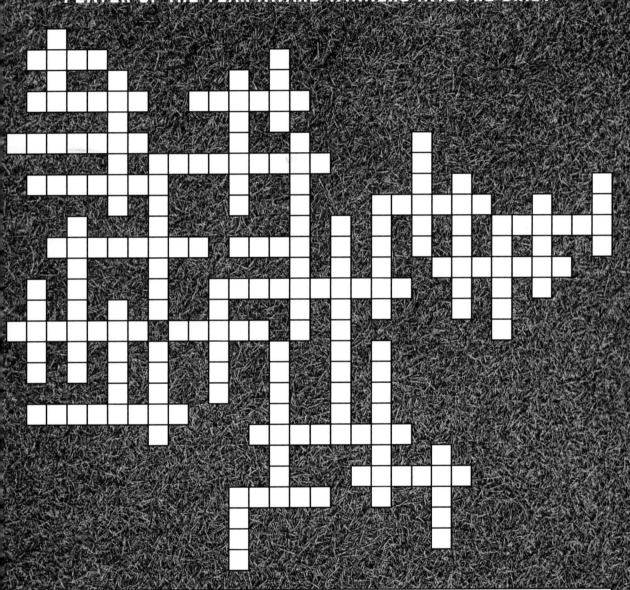

4 Letters
Cort
Dann
Shaw
Wood
Zaha

5 Letters
Boyce
Bryan
Clyne

Jones
Thorn
Zhiyi

6 Letters
Barron
Bright
Cannon
Hincks
Hopkin
Murphy

Sansom
Taylor
Thomas
Wright

7 Letters
Coleman
Gilbert
Jedinak
Johnson
Mullins

Roberts
Speroni

8 Letters
Edworthy
Freedman
Holdaway
Jeffries
Kikomeko
Linighan
Mitchell

9 Letters
McCormick

10 Letters
McGoldrick
WanBissaka

11 Letters
Hinshelwood

Solution on p61

PALACE GOODBYE:
JASON PUNCHEON AND JONNY WILLIAMS

At the end of last season, we said goodbye to two long-serving players who provided over 23 years of service between them – midfielders Jason Puncheon and Jonny Williams.

Local boy Jason first joined the club on loan from Southampton in 2013, before moving permanently back to south London in January 2014.

The former captain scored 16 goals in 169 Palace appearances, including the 2016 FA Cup Final opener against Manchester United.

"To have had the honour of captaining the club, my club, the club I supported as a boy, will always remain with me as one of my proudest achievements. I've loved every minute of my time at Palace," he said.

Academy graduate and Welsh international midfielder Jonny left the Eagles after 17 years at the club, having joined as an eight-year-old.

After making his debut in August 2011, he went on to help gain promotion to the Premier League and win the Crystal Palace Young Player of the Year Award, scoring once in 70 appearances for Palace.

QUIZ ANSWERS

SPOT THE BALL ANSWER – PAGE 41

WORDSEARCH ANSWERS – PAGE 19

B	V	M	C	B	K	N	V	J	N	K	D	Q	X	T	H	J	K	Z	L	K			
R	T	Y	P	G	W	E	S	T	H	A	M	U	N	I	T	E	D	F	R	D			
I	N	L	T	Y	B	B	N	P	M	R	K	M	P	R	U	B	B	Z	R	T			
G	Z	P	T	I	N	Y	U	T	G	N	Y	F	Q	D	O	G	S	M	U	Z			
H	X	Z	M	Y	C	N	D	R	O	F	T	A	W	R	M	L	H	A	P	L			
T	B	L	W	R	K	R	C	M	N	Y	T	N	M	V	E	V	E	N	S	R			
O	L	N	L	N	S	H	E	K	R	L	L	G	R	K	N	R	F	C	T	B			
N	P	Z	K	J	E	O	K	T	N	H	E	L	F	F	R	K	F	H	O	G			
A	B	D	R	L	N	L	U	D	S	V	T	Y	R	Y	U	L	I	E	H	N			
N	Z	R	S	F	Z	D	B	T	B	E	B	B	T	M	O	O	E	S	M	P			
D	K	E	J	B	J	M	C	F	H	T	C	I	R	L	B	O	L	T	A	D			
A	S	T	O	N	V	I	L	L	A	C	I	A	H	C	P	D	E	H	H			
O	T	T	X	B	X	H	T	F	Q	H	M	N	E	L	F	R	U	R	N	T			
E	L	V	L	J	R	X	W	I	D	S	M	W	T	P	C	V	I	I	T	C			
A	T	T	L	T	B	O	W	X	R	N	G	T	Y	Q	N	F	H	U	L	E			
L	P	T	M	Z	L	R	Y	A	T	Y	Q	N	F	M	X	L	L	E	Y	O	Z		
B	G	Z	Y	V	O	M	M	D	K	Y	M	L	Z	L	N	K	D	Q	T	D			
I	P	V	E	N	Z	N	N	K	M	D	B	R	Y	N	O	T	R	E	V	E			
O	H	S	X	B	L	N	E	W	C	A	S	T	L	E	U	N	I	T	E	D			
N	N	R	M	A	N	C	H	E	S	T	E	R	U	N	I	T	E	D	N	C			

WORDFIT ANSWERS – PAGE 59

			Z																					
P	A	R	R								R		S											
S	A	N	S	O	M			J			T	H	O	M	A	S								
											B		W											
M	U	L	L	I	N	S					E			M							M			
						S		M	C	C	O	R	M	I	C	K					U			
S	P	E	R	O	N	I						G		O			H	O	P	K	I	N		
		K					T					O		L			I			B				
	L	I	N	I	G	H	A	N		W	O	O	D				N			B	A	R	R	O	N
		T					T							R			C				Y			
		T			W	A	N	B	I	S	S	A	K	A			S							
C	O	L	E	M	A	N		Z	H	I	Y	I												
	R				R																			
J	E	F	F	R	I	E	S																	
									F	R	E	E	D	M	A	N								
																		C	A	N	N	O	N	
	C	L	Y	N	E